PIANO · VOCAL · GUITAR

come away with me

ISBN 0-634-05264-0

7777 W. BLUEMOUND RD. P.O. BOX 13819 MILWAUKEE, WI 53213

Visit Hal Leonard Online at
www.halleonard.com

DON'T KNOW WHY

Words and Music by
JESSE HARRIS

SEVEN YEARS

Words and Music by
LEE ALEXANDER

COLD COLD HEART

Words and Music by
HANK WILLIAMS

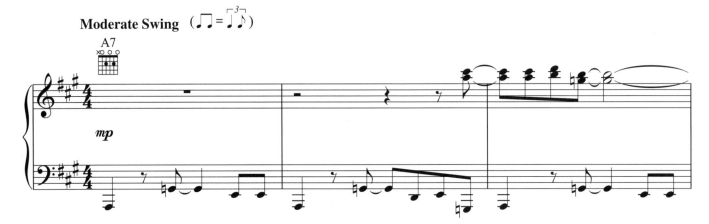

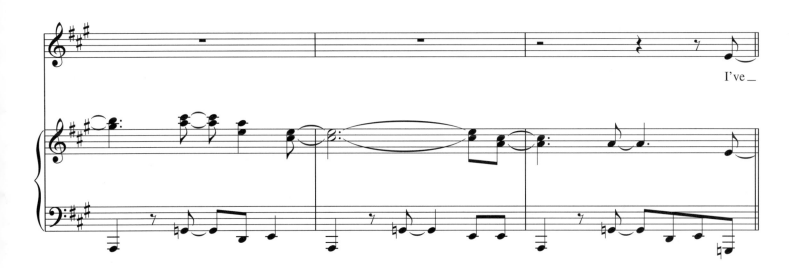

* An optional ending is provided.

FEELIN' THE SAME WAY

Words and Music by
LEE ALEXANDER

Moderate Rock

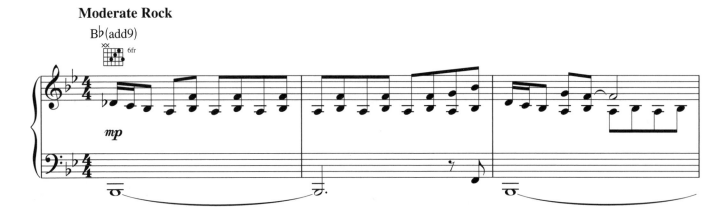

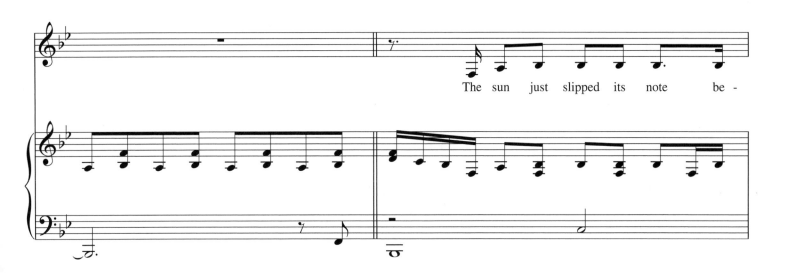

The sun just slipped its note be-

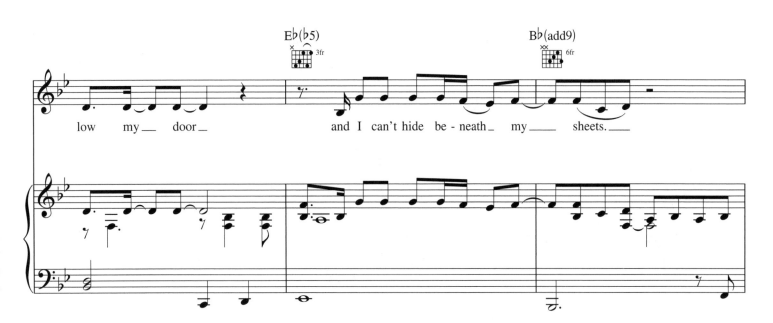

low my door and I can't hide be-neath my sheets.

COME AWAY WITH ME

Words and Music by
NORAH JONES

SHOOT THE MOON

Words and Music by
JESSE HARRIS

Moderately slow

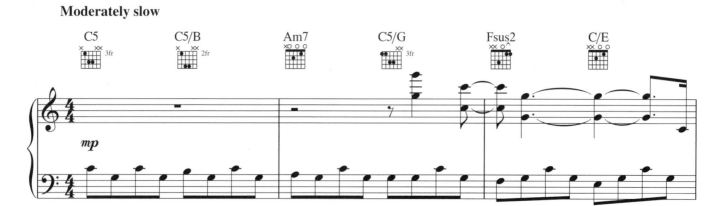

The sum-mer days ___ are gone ___ too soon.

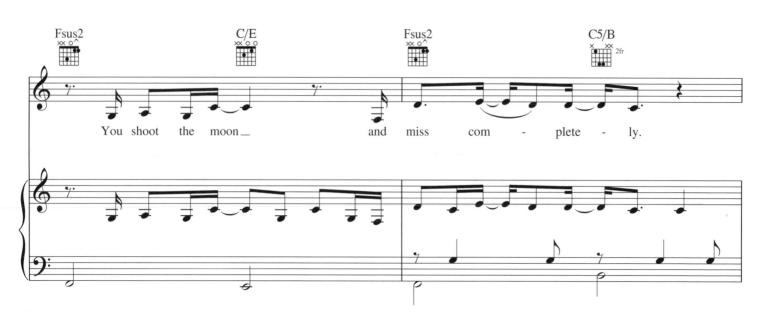

You shoot the moon ___ and miss com - plete - ly.

TURN ME ON

Words and Music by
JOHN. D. LOUDERMILK

LONESTAR

Words and Music by
LEE ALEXANDER

I pick up _____ a stone _____ that I _____ cast _____ to the

sky, _____ hop - in' _____ for some kind of _____ sign. _____

Lone - star, _____ where are _____ you ____ out ___ to - night? This

I'VE GOT TO SEE YOU AGAIN

Words and Music by
JESSE HARRIS

Moderately slow Rhumba

Lines _____ on your face _____ don't both-

PAINTER SONG

Words and Music by LEE ALEXANDER
and J.C. HOPKINS

ONE FLIGHT DOWN

Words and Music by
JESSE HARRIS

One flight down there's a song ___ on ___

Original key: D♭ major. This edition has been transposed up one half-step to be more playable.

NIGHTINGALE

Words and Music by
NORAH JONES

(Guitar solo ad-lib.)

All the voic - es that are spin-nin' a - round_

(Piano solo-ad lib.)

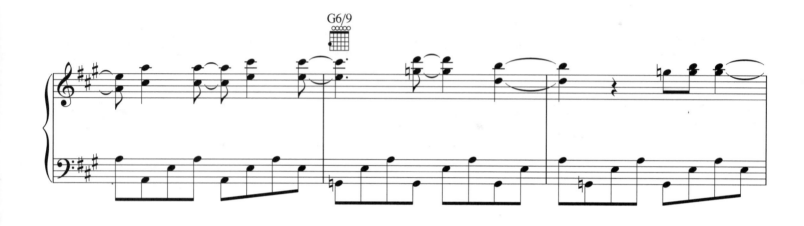

Optional Ending

Repeat and Fade

THE LONG DAY IS OVER

Words and Music by NORAH JONES
and JESSE HARRIS

THE NEARNESS OF YOU

from the Paramount Picture ROMANCE IN THE DARK

Words by NED WASHINGTON
Music by HOAGY CARMICHAEL